THE OCTOPUS

BY
CARL R. GREEN
WILLIAM R. SANFORD

EDITED BY
JUDY LOCKWOOD

PUBLISHED BY
CRESTWOOD HOUSE
Mankato, MN, U.S.A.

LIBRARY OF CONGRESS CATALOGING IN PUBLICATION DATA

Green, Carl R.
 The octopus

 (Wildlife, habits & habitat)
 Includes index.
 SUMMARY: Examines the physical characteristics, behavior, lifestyle, and natural environment of the octopus.
  1. Octopus—Juvenile literature. [1. Octopus.] I. Sanford, William R. (William Reynolds), 1927-   . II. Lockwood, Judy. III. Title. IV. Series.
 QL430.3.02G74   1988   594'.56—dc19   88-5435
 ISBN 0-89686-386-7

International Standard Book Number:	Library of Congress Catalog Card Number:
0-89686-386-7	88-5435

PHOTO CREDITS:

Cover: Tom Stack & Associates: Gary Milburn
Tom Stack & Associates: (Gary Milburn) 4, 13, 22, 40;
 (F. Stuart Westmorland) 7, 11, 25, 43; (Ed Robinson) 8, 33, 34, 38; (Brian Parker) 15, 17; (Carl Roessler) 18, 21; (Neil G. McDaniel) 26; (Tom Stack) 29; (David M. Dennis) 30

Produced by Carnival Enterprises.

CRESTWOOD HOUSE

Box 3427, Mankato, MN, U.S.A. 56002

TABLE OF CONTENTS

Despite their scary shape, octopuses are quiet, peaceful animals.

INTRODUCTION:

Andrew held tightly to his mother's hand as he looked around the aquarium. In the big tanks, brightly-colored fish were swimming lazily through tropical coral reefs. A moray eel glided silently along the sandy bottom.

Suddenly, Andrew pulled his mother to a nearby tank. "Look," he cried, "there's an octopus!" The strange-looking creature was climbing slowly up a

4

rock wall. Each of the animal's eight arms seemed to move with a life of its own. As Andrew and his mother watched, the octopus changed from a dark red to a pale grey color.

Andrew's sister, Eileen, put her free hand over her eyes. "I can't stand creepy, squishy things like that," she said with a shudder.

Andrew put his nose against the glass. "The octopus can't help how it looks," he told his mother. "Besides, this is only a small one. I saw a movie last week that showed a giant octopus attacking a submarine. That octopus was a hundred times bigger!"

Eileen read the card posted beside the tank. "Maybe the filmmakers were playing tricks on you," she said. "It says here that the world's biggest octopus is *octopus hongkongensis.* That one is only about 30 feet (9 meters) from tip to tip. Despite all that 'arm' span, their bodies are only 18 inches (46 centimeters) long. That doesn't sound big enough to eat a submarine."

Andrew frowned as he thought about that. Then he smiled. "Well, maybe an octopus could gobble up a scuba diver every once in a while!"

"I'm sorry, that only happens in bad movies," a deep voice broke in. A smiling, bearded man was standing beside them. "I'd be glad to tell you a little about the octopus. I've been studying them ever since I joined the staff here. My name is Kit."

"Do you mean the octopus never attacks people?" Andrew asked.

Kit nodded. "There's nothing vicious about an octopus," he said. "It will wrap its arms around someone who invades its habitat, mostly out of curiosity. If the swimmer tries to pull away, the octopus just holds on tighter and tighter. That's how scuba divers get their masks or air hoses ripped off. If you stand still for a little while, the octopus will soon let go."

"Are you saying that the octopus never hurts humans?" Eileen asked. She didn't sound convinced.

"Most octopuses are shy, nearly harmless creatures," Kit replied. "The exception is an octopus that is deadlier than a cobra. The blue-ringed octopus lives in Australian coastal waters. It is only four inches (10 cm) across, but its bite can kill a person in five minutes. People pick it up because it's pretty, but that can be a fatal mistake."

"How about this octopus?" Eileen pointed to the tank.

"This is the common octopus," Kit said. "Even if it bit you, the bite wouldn't be any worse than a bee sting. In fact, scientists have found chemicals in the saliva of the octopus that may someday save lives. One chemical helps keep blood from clotting, and another controls high blood pressure."

Andrew watched the octopus slip into a narrow crack in the rocks. "I read somewhere that octopuses

If a diver is gentle, he can come quite close to a giant octopus without getting hurt.

are smart," he said. "This one doesn't look very smart to me."

"The experts say that octopuses have the best brains of any mollusk or fish," Kit said with a smile. "Only whales, dolphins, and other seagoing mammals are smarter. Now, I'd better get to work. It's time to feed my friends here."

"Thanks for telling us about octopuses," Andrew said.

After Kit left, Andrew turned to his mother. "Let's buy a book on octopuses before we leave," he begged. "I want to know all about them before we make our next visit to the aquarium."

CHAPTER ONE:

Millions of years ago, the oceans were filled with the ancestors of today's octopus and squid. Unlike the fish and whales that took their place, these *cephalopods* were invertebrates (creatures without backbones). Although they were mollusks like clams and snails, most of the cephalopods lost their outside shells. The mollusk's single "foot" became a cluster of strong, grasping arms. In addition, cephalopods developed larger brains and the ability to move about freely in the water.

Octopuses live in most of the world's oceans. They avoid only the deepest and coldest waters.

The cephalopods that survived are the octopus, squid, cuttlefish, pearly nautilus, and spirula. Of these, only the pearly nautilus still has its outer shell. The name "cephalopod" comes from the Greek word meaning "feet around the head." If you look closely at an octopus, you'll see that its eight arms do surround its mouth. Cephalopods are found in all the world's oceans, from the Arctic Sea to the edge of the Antarctic ice shelf. Most octopuses live in shallow water. One Antarctic species, however, is found at depths ranging from a few feet to more than two miles (3 kilometers).

A large and varied family

Of the 650 different cephalopods that have survived, about 150 are octopuses. The family name for these animals is *octopoda*. The squid, a close relative, has two long tentacles besides its eight arms.

The octopods vary greatly in size. *Octopus arborescens* measures only two inches (5 cm) from tip to tip. A record octopus hongkongensis may stretch out to 32 feet (10 m) and weigh 100 pounds (45 kilograms) or more. Most of its weight is in its arms. The body of a big octopus isn't much larger than a basketball!

Octopods vary in other ways, too. The one-half

inch (1.3 cm) male argonaut is only one-twentieth the size of the female. Another relative, the blind cirrothauma, has two fins and lives in the deepest parts of the ocean.

The best known octopod is the common octopus. The common octopus sometimes grows as large as ten feet (3 m) across, but is usually much smaller. It is found in the Atlantic Ocean and Mediterranean Sea, ranging from tropical waters to Great Britain's southern coast. A smaller octopus ranges down the coast of Europe from Norway to the Mediterranean. North America's largest octopus is the common Pacific octopus, which can grow as large as 28 feet (8.5 m) across.

A head and body all in one

The head and body of the octopus are really one unit. The head is attached to the soft, bag-shaped body by a short, almost invisible "neck." Inside the body lie two small, soft "bones." These are the only reminders that the octopus once had a hard shell like other mollusks. The thick outer skin, called the mantle, is covered with bumps that look like large warts. The mantle is connected on three sides at the "neck," leaving it free to expand and contract.

Large, bulbous eyes stick up from the head. The

The common Pacific octopus is the largest North American octopus.

mouth is hidden on the underside, surrounded by the eight arms. Inside the mouth opening is a strong, curved beak. An octopus can break through the shells of clams, lobsters, crabs, and other shellfish with its beak. The mouth also contains a tongue that works like a file. Small, hooked teeth cut the octopus's prey into edible bits as the tongue saws back and forth and sideways.

Making good use of eight arms

The octopus makes good use of its eight arms. The long, flexible arms branch out from the body like an eight-pointed star. A fold of skin forms a web-like membrane where the arms meet the body. Two rows of suction discs on each arm help the octopus scale a rock wall or hold tight to its prey. The discs are largest near the middle of the arm. The common octopus has 240 discs on each arm, and it can control each disc separately.

The discs work like suction cups. When the octopus wraps its arms around something and draws up on the center of each disc, a vacuum is created. The pressure of the water on the outside of the discs holds them in place. In one experiment, it took more than 500 pounds (227 kg) of force to break the grip of a

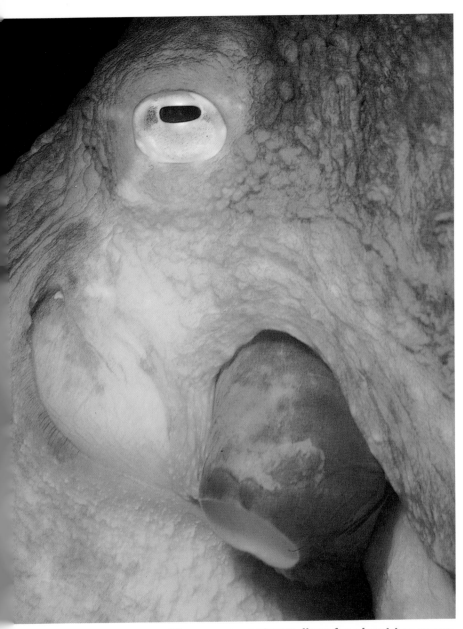

The average octopus lives for about two years.

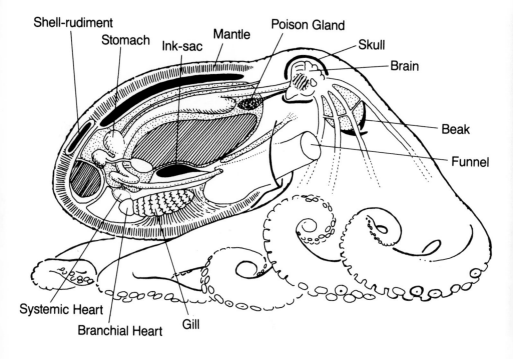

Shell-rudiment
Stomach
Ink-sac
Mantle
Poison Gland
Skull
Brain
Beak
Funnel
Systemic Heart
Branchial Heart
Gill

five-foot (1.5-m) octopus. The discs also give the octopus a well-developed sense of touch. It uses its discs to examine food before it feeds.

Breathing and swimming

An octopus has gills for breathing, much as fish do. As the mantle expands, water flows across the gills. The gills take oxygen from the water. When the mantle contracts, the water is pumped out again. Two

14

A web-like membrane attaches an octopus's arms to its body.

of the octopus's three hearts pump blood to the gills, where it picks up the new oxygen supply. The third heart pumps the blood to the octopus's body and arms.

The mantle also plays a role in the octopus's unusual method of swimming. With a gentle flap of its mantle, the octopus propels itself through the water, arms trailing behind. For faster speeds, it adds jet propulsion! When the octopus closes its mantle, water squirts out of a nozzle-like device called the funnel. The force of the water jet moves the octopus as fast as eight miles (13 km) per hour.

A well-developed brain

Naturalists say that the octopus has the best brain of all the invertebrates. Its ability to survive in a dangerous habitat is one proof. To test that brain, a captive octopus named Lee was shown a shrimp in a corked bottle. After a little practice, Lee learned to uncork the bottle to get to the shrimp!

Along with its good brain, the octopus has excellent eyesight. Its large eyes are similar to the human eye, with a cornea, iris, lens, and retina. Because its eyes stand up on rounded knobs, the octopus has a full 360 degree range of vision. If the octopus loses part of an eye, it can regrow the missing part.

The octopus's other senses are still rather mysterious. Blind octopuses, studies show, depend more on taste than on touch to find food. The octopus's entire skin surface is lined with receptors that react to chemicals in the water. An organ that might give the octopus a sense of smell is located near the eyes, but little is known about it. No one knows whether octopuses have a sense of hearing.

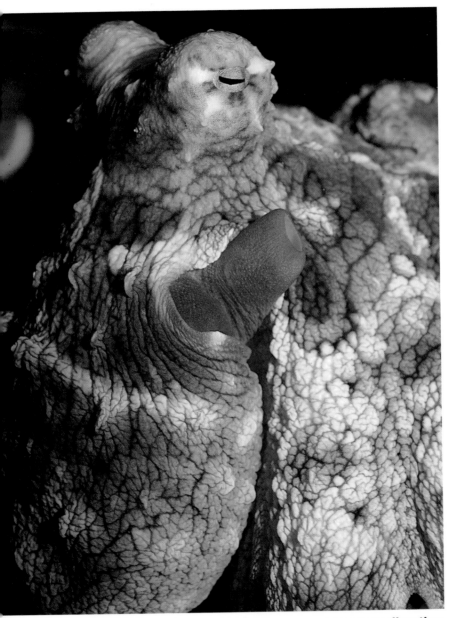

An octopus's large, round eyes can see in every direction.

A creature of many colors

Each octopus has a basic color. The common octopus, for example, is greyish-white on the underside and yellow-brown on top. You may never see those colors, however, because the octopus changes color whenever it wishes. Thousands of black, brown, red, yellow, or red-orange color cells called chromatophores (pronounced kro-MAT-uh-foers) lie just under the skin. Only three of these colors are found in any one octopus. Reflective cells known

Octopuses can change colors to blend in perfectly with their surroundings.

as iridocytes (pronounced ih-RID-o-sites) add a shimmering, glowing look to the changing colors.

The octopus creates its rainbow of color effects by expanding or contracting each tiny cell. Colors move in waves across the skin as the cells expand up to 3,000 times their original size. Naturalists say that color changes reflect the octopus's mood. Danger causes it to turn pale, and excitement causes it to blush a deep rose. To hide, the octopus changes both its color and its skin texture. Even skilled divers have trouble finding an octopus when it is blending in perfectly with its habitat.

CHAPTER TWO:

Like its earliest ancestors, the octopus ranges through most of the world's oceans. It avoids only the deepest and the coldest waters. The octopus prefers shallow, coastal habitats, but a few species live two miles (3 km) or more below the surface. Although the octopus swims well, it spends most of its time on the bottom.

Some octopuses change their habitat with the seasons. In the Mediterranean, full-grown common octopuses move inshore from the deeper water during the colder months. The males tend to swim inshore earlier than the females.

A lonely life

The octopus lives a solitary life on the ocean floor. Most octopuses pick lairs where they are hidden from sight. Even if other octopuses live nearby, they come together only when they mate. If an octopus finds a big empty shell, a piece of wreckage, or an old bottle, it will set up housekeeping. At other times, an octopus will bury itself in sand or mud. To make itself feel safer, it often piles rocks in front of its lair. Some octopuses give their hiding places away by leaving the shells of their prey near the entrance.

An octopus slips easily into cracks and holes that look much too small for it. To do so, it compresses its boneless body into almost any shape or size. In one experiment, an octopus named Billie squeezed through a half-inch (1.3-cm) hole. Billie's arm span was over 12 inches (30 cm), and her body was the size of a tennis ball. In an even more incredible feat, an octopus the same size worked its way out of a closed cigar box. The cephalopod escaped even though the box was tacked shut!

Hunting by night

Octopuses feed mainly on shellfish such as crabs and lobsters. They also eat other mollusks, including clams, oysters, and scallops. When it's hungry, the

Small bumps that look like warts cover the octopus's mantle.

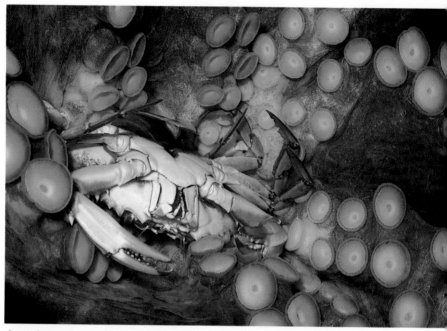

A crab can not escape the powerful arms of an octopus.

octopus is a patient and deadly hunter. It leaves its lair at night and lies in wait for its prey to appear. Silent and motionless, it can wait for hours without losing patience. On another night, the octopus might creep across the ocean floor, "walking" on its eight arms like a spider. Another trick is to float near the surface like a jellyfish. When an unwary lobster walks underneath, the octopus spreads its arms and descends on its prey.

Few animals escape the grasp of the octopus. The powerful arms pull the victim close to the octopus's mouth and its sharp beak. A single bite usually breaks through a tough shell, killing the prey. The octopus doesn't rely only on its beak, however. Two glands close to the beak produce a poison that kills almost instantly. Naturalists believe that the octopus doesn't have to inject the poison into its prey. Caught in the closed space under the mantle, the prey breathes in the deadly fluid. The octopus's poison also softens the victim's flesh. This allows the octopus to extract every bit of meat from a crab's claw without breaking the entire shell open.

A dangerous life

Naturalists seldom find parasites in the octopus, and few suffer from disease. Even so, the life of an octopus is full of peril. Predators of varying sizes feed on the octopus at each stage of its life. Crabs and small fish like to dine on octopus eggs. Later on, newborn octopuses are fair game for almost any fish that finds them. Larger octopuses must be watchful for sharks, toothed whales, seals, and eels.

The moray eel is the most deadly of all the predators that hunt the octopus. Unlike larger fish, the moray can invade the rocks where octopuses hide. A muscular, six-foot (1.8-m) moray can grab an octopus's arm and twist until it tears off. If it succeeds, the moray returns again and again until the octopus is dead. The octopus doesn't lose all of these battles. It sometimes gets in a killing bite with its beak, or it may escape by jetting away in a cloud of ink.

When caught by an arm, an octopus sometimes "sheds" that arm. Lizards lose their tails in a similar way, but the octopus's arm may separate anywhere along its length. After the loss, an octopus doesn't bleed. Nearby blood vessels contract and seal off the flow of blood from the injury. Six weeks after losing one-third of an arm, a common octopus will have regrown the missing section.

An inky getaway

The octopus isn't fast enough to rely on speed to escape from predators. Instead, it squirts out a cloud of ink that covers its getaway. Octopus ink can be brown, purple, or black. The liquid ink is stored in a pear-shaped ink sac. Located between the gills, the sac discharges its contents through a long tube that ends in the funnel. The sac holds enough ink to allow several "shots" in a row, and it's ready for use at any time. When scientists found dried octopus ink in million-year-old fossils, they put a chunk in water. After the ink dissolved, the scientists were able to use it for writing letters!

Naturalists say that the ink is more than a smoke-screen. The octopus often mixes the ink with mucus, so that it hangs longer in the water. The resulting ink cloud looks very much like an octopus! A pursuer will attack the inky decoy, giving the octopus time to

hen an octopus is frightened, it squirts out a cloud of ink that confuses
s enemy.

escape. Studies also show that the ink spoils the moray eel's sense of smell. Since the moray hunts mostly by scent, the octopus has time to find a safe hiding place.

Besides the ink, the octopus's safety depends on its ability to camouflage itself. If it's on a white, sandy bottom, the octopus turns pale and sandy looking. Moved to a rocky ledge, it takes on a mottled, rocky look. To complete the illusion, the skin of the mantle forms itself into rough ridges. When threatened, the octopus often turns a pale white on one side. The other half, however, may remain a dark red! Naturalists have seen octopuses with streaks and wavy bands of

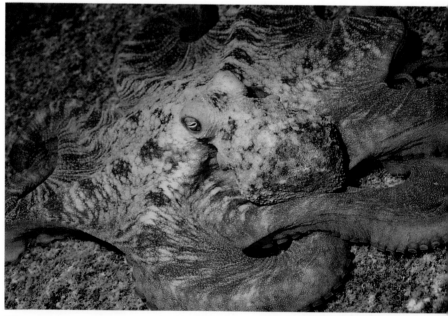

The octopus spends most of its life by itself in shallow, coastal waters.

26

color, including purple polka dots. For all its color changing ability, the octopus is unable to turn a true red or a true blue.

A shy, gentle animal

The average octopus lives about two years if it survives the first dangerous months. Despite its scary looks, the octopus is a shy, almost gentle animal. When it encounters a larger animal, it flees or hides. Left to itself, the octopus seems content to live out a quiet, solitary life cycle.

CHAPTER THREE:

The scuba divers drift slowly along the rocky ocean floor just off the Florida Keys. They smile with pleasure as schools of silvery fish streak past. Suddenly, the woman puts her hand on the man's shoulder and points. As he looks down, a jagged rock seems to move! The rock "grows" arms and a pair of cold, unblinking eyes. The divers have spotted a female common octopus.

The frightened octopus jets quickly towards her lair, leaving a half-eaten lobster behind. A moment later, she slips into a narrow crevice in a jumble of rocks.

A quiet courtship

The female octopus watches the scuba divers swim away in a cloud of bubbles. Then she forgets the intruders. Another octopus is creeping towards her lair. One extra-large suction disc marks him as a male. The female pulls back farther into her hole, but the male knows she's there. He extends his third right arm and gently strokes the female. As she feels the touch of the spoon-shaped tip, pleasure replaces fear. Waves of red and brown wash across her body. The male reaches under her mantle and continues his stroking. The two-year-old female is mating for the first and last time.

The two octopuses hold their arms-length embrace for many hours. The male turns a pale blue as small bundles of sperm cells slide along a groove in his arm. The sperm enter the female's body through an opening near her funnel. Finally, the female pushes the male away from her. He swims away on the current, never to return.

Spawning is a big job

The female doesn't lay her eggs right away. She feeds well in the days that follow, preparing for the

Newly-laid octopus eggs hang from the walls of an underwater cave.

work ahead. Three weeks later, she moves into a small cave not far from shore. The opening to her nursery cave is only an inch (2 cm) wide. Her softball-sized body squeezes through easily. Once inside, she gathers stones and piles them up to block the entrance.

It's time for her to lay her eggs, a process known as spawning. As the eggs emerge from her egg tube, they are fertilized by the male's sperm. Each egg looks like a tiny grain of rice with a long, silky thread sticking to it. The female gathers the eggs by their threads and glues them into bunches. Each bunch contains about 1,000 eggs. When she's finished two weeks later, the female has 50,000 eggs hanging from the walls of her cave and that isn't even the record. A captive common octopus once produced 180,000 eggs in an aquarium tank!

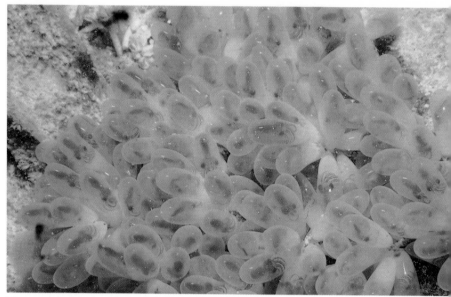

Tiny octopuses show through their delicate eggs.

Weeks of guard duty

Day after day, the female cares for her eggs. Keeping them safe from predators is only part of her job. She blows water over them, and cleans them with her smallest sucker discs. If sand or parasites collect on the eggs, they won't hatch. The octopus is on duty 24 hours a day.

When the eggs are a few weeks old, a pair of black eyes show through each thin wall. The female brushes against the nearest bunch, and the unborn octopuses flush a bright orange-brown. Their color cells are already working.

Hungry fish are waiting outside the crevice. The smaller ones would invade the nursery if the female left the eggs unguarded. The octopus hasn't eaten for over a week, nor will she eat again. A crab crawls by the opening to the lair, but she ignores it. Nothing that could harm the eggs is allowed inside the cave. The long fast has weakened her. Some females die before the eggs hatch.

Only a few survive

Fifty days after spawning, the eggs begin to hatch. The female has done her job well. Almost every egg produces a tiny octopus. The hatch, as they're called, are less than one-eighth inch (3 millimeters) long. They're covered with a crown of fine hair and their arms are tiny stubs. The hair helps keep them afloat as they drift with the current.

As the eggs hatch, the female must watch her brood drift away. The waiting fish snap them up in great mouthfuls. Almost at once, 10,000 of the hatch are eaten. When the last bunch of eggs has hatched, the female is too weak to leave the crevice. She dies five days later.

For the next several weeks, the hatch float at the upper level of the ocean. Little is known about this stage of their life, except that more perish every day. Most are eaten. Others are washed into a tidepool and die when the tide leaves them behind. Finally, the survivors swim to the sea floor. Their arms are growing, and they've lost their crown of fine hair. They're beginning to look like tiny adults.

The octopus grows up

At two months, the young octopuses have found homes on the ocean floor. They stay in shallow water, where food is easier to find. They are much too small to kill a lobster or large crab. There are plenty of tiny shellfish for these patient hunters, however. Their weight is increasing rapidly. When food is plentiful, they can double their weight in a week.

Life is still dangerous for the growing octopuses. Those who don't stay hidden end up in the stomachs of the fish that cruise the area. A scuba diver gathers up a bucketful to use as bait. Another 100 find out too late that big octopuses eat small octopuses. A four-year-old male catches them before they can scramble into their holes.

To escape predators, an octopus can slip in and out of small cracks and holes.

When summer comes again, only 15 of the hatch are still alive. Eight of them die quickly when a moray eel moves into the area. The others find deeper crevices and hide from the deadly, needle-sharp teeth of the eel. A week later, the moray catches sight of the biggest surviving female. As the eel swims in for the kill, the octopus shoots out a cloud of black ink. The ink hangs in the water and confuses the moray, who circles it as if it were the octopus. By the time the water clears, the female is safely back in her lair.

Octopuses float near the top of the water and swoop down to catch lobsters walking on the ocean floor.

A sudden change of habitat

The female is fond of fiddler crabs. One evening, she chases some crabs onto the nearby beach. Being out of the water for a short time doesn't bother her. She creeps quickly across the damp sand, catching crabs and holding them with her suckers.

A boy sees the octopus and runs to pick her up. The octopus drops her crabs and wraps her arms about his wrist. The suckers feel like tiny, wet hands pulling at his skin. Each time he pulls an arm loose, the others grip tighter. The struggle ends when the octopus bites the boy's arm. Stung and frightened, the boy rips her loose and flings her back into the sea.

Five minutes later, the octopus crawls back into her lair. Unlike most octopuses, she has survived her first contact with humans.

CHAPTER FOUR:

Humans have mixed feelings about the octopus. To some people, the octopus is a "devilfish." They say this eight-armed cephalopod looks like an evil alien from outer space. Other people like the octopus. Ancient artists, for example, painted octopuses on walls and pottery. They even gave it a place of honor on their coins.

A creature that inspires legends

The octopus appears in many old legends. The Greek poet Homer wrote about Odysseus and his fight with a many-headed sea monster named Scylla. Every time Odysseus cut off a head, Scylla grew a new one. Modern readers believe that Homer was describing a huge octopus.

In the 1880s, authors invented sea monsters to make their books more exciting. Victor Hugo describes a fight to the death between his hero and a "devilfish" in *The Toilers of the Sea*.

Real life adventures

Explorer Thor Heyerdahl writes of his real-life adventure with an octopus in *Kon-Tiki*. After his raft ran onto a Pacific reef, Heyerdahl had to wade ashore. As he splashed through the shallow water, an octopus caught him by both ankles. It was only a small octopus, but Heyerdahl couldn't pull it loose. Finally, he managed to drag the creature up to the beach. In a similar incident, an octopus grabbed an English woman as she was wading in the Mediterranean. The five-foot (1.5-m) octopus pinned her to the spot. If friends hadn't rescued her, she might have drowned when the tide came in.

Experts say an octopus which grabs someone is only curious. If you remain quiet, the octopus will let you go after it examines you. That's hard to do, because instinct tells you to pull yourself free. In one such tug-of-war, an octopus was too strong for the three sailors who were trying to pull a deep sea diver from its grasp. The desperate men saved their friend by tying the rope which was fastened to the diver to their ship as it dipped down on a wave. When the ship rose on the next wave, they yanked the diver and the octopus free of the bottom.

Some people eat octopus

The tough, rubbery meat of the octopus is a favorite food in many parts of the world. Each slice must be pounded until it's tender. In most dishes, the chef cooks the meat in oils and spices. Mexicans are fond of octopus that's been cooked in its own ink, and the Japanese say the eyes are tasty. The Greeks, Turks, and Polynesian people enjoy small octopuses that have been dried in the sun.

People who fish for octopus catch them in many different ways. The ancient Egyptians lowered clay pots into places in the sea where they knew octopuses lived. When they pulled up each pot a week later, they often found an octopus living inside. Modern octopus fishers use nets baited with crabs, or lead bars covered with hooks. Mexicans lower a crab on a line to the bottom, and haul up the octopus when it grabs the bait.

An unusual use for the octopus

About 1900, the Japanese used the octopus as a salvage diver. To recover valuable bowls from a sunken ship, they lowered an octopus on the end of a line. When the octopus crawled into a bowl, the men pulled octopus and bowl to the surface. People on the island of Crete in southern Greece salvaged coal in the same way after World War II. A supply of the scarce fuel lay on the harbor floor where it had fallen from coal-burning ships. When an octopus was lowered to

Scientists have seen octopuses colored in shades of red, white, purple, and blue.

the bottom, it grabbed instinctively at the loose coal. The Cretans then pulled the octopus to the surface and collected lumps of coal from its suckers!

Today, most people are content to let this strange sea creature alone. Some naturalists disagree. They are intrigued by the octopus, and devote their lives to learning more about it.

CHAPTER FIVE:

Joanne Duffy is bright, athletic, and pretty. When people hear about her unusual job, they seem surprised.

Joanne is a diver and marine biologist. Her special passion is the giant octopus that lives in Washington state's Puget Sound. On a working day, Joanne may put on scuba gear and dive into the cold waters near Port Townsend. She skims along the ocean floor, looking for an octopus that might be hiding under the huge logs dumped there by logging companies.

When Joanne finds an octopus, she sticks her arm into its lair. After she drives the octopus into the open, she wrestles it to the surface. Some of these giant octopuses weigh 125 pounds (57 kg). Jacques Cousteau, the famous deep sea diver, has watched her work. He says that Joanne handles the octopuses "as though they were trained dogs in a circus."

Octopuses are slow-moving animals that rarely attack people.

A career as a diver

As a child in Montana, Joanne liked to swim and watch films about the sea. She had never seen the ocean before her family moved to Seattle, Washington, but it was love at first sight. She took up scuba diving and became an expert.

One of Joanne's first adventures with octopuses came in 1967. Seattle was holding an octopus-catching contest. The winner would become the World Champion Octopus Diver (that was probably a safe claim, because no other city was holding a contest of this type!).

Joanne knew that the giant octopuses lived under the logs that lay scattered on the bottom. At first she was afraid to swim under the logs. What if an octopus dropped on her? In time, she realized that the slow-moving creatures wouldn't attack her. She caught some octopuses and began to learn more about them.

Rules for handling a giant octopus

In time, Joanne became an expert on the giant octopus. The first thing she learned was that it's a hard animal to find. She swam past many hidden octopuses without seeing them. If they're lying in a bed of kelp, for example, they take on the color and texture of the seaweed.

Joanne taught divers how to react if they become tangled with one of the big cephalopods. An angry octopus can rip off a diver's mask or pull out his breathing tube. Joanne says that a diver should hold the octopus's body at arm's length and rock it from side to side. The octopus will relax and loosen its grip. When it's calm, the diver can lay it on its side. If a diver is nervous, the octopus will sense it. A frightened octopus thinks only of escape.

Joanne's students worry about the octopus's sharp, strong beak. When asked about the danger, Joanne doesn't recall anyone being bitten. In order to bite, she says, an octopus must bring its victim close to its beak. A diver can prevent this by holding the body at arm's length. The octopus's ink doesn't bother Joanne, either. She knows that the animal will stop squirting as soon as she calms it down.

Octopus on display

One of Joanne's jobs was to show the giant octopus to visitors at an oceanarium. Joanne first worked with each animal until it felt safe around her. After that, the

To keep octopuses calm, divers hold them at arms length and rock them gently.

octopus would do almost anything for its new friend.

Joanne was impressed by the cephalopod's learning ability. To do the show, she had to take an octopus from its lair and carry it to the window for viewing. After a few shows, the octopus seemed to know the schedule. When Joanne swam to its lair, it was waiting for her. As soon as she tickled its arms, the octopus swam directly to the window. Joanne didn't have to reward it with bits of food. She thinks the octopus performed because it enjoyed doing the show.

The performing octopuses didn't like everybody. Divers who handled them roughly soon found the octopuses wouldn't work for them. Despite its size and scary looks, the octopus is a delicate animal. It goes into a state of shock or nervous collapse if someone hurts it.

Friends, not aliens

People often ask Joanne about her love of the giant octopus. "They seem to be very intelligent and sensitive," she says, "and yet very different from us. I want to protect them, to keep them from being hurt." Joanne Duffy is as good as her word. She is working hard to make sure the octopus will be with us for a long time to come.

MAP:

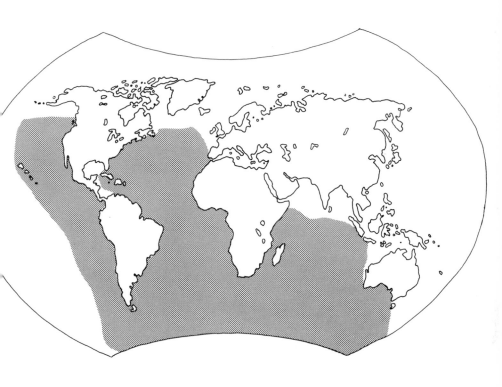

Most octopuses live in these areas.

INDEX/GLOSSARY:

INDEX/GLOSSARY:

WILDLIFE
HABITS & HABITAT

READ AND ENJOY THE SERIES:

If you would like to know more about all kinds of wildlife, you should take a look at the other books in this series.

You'll find books on bald eagles and other birds. Books on alligators and other reptiles. There are books about deer and other big-game animals. And there are books about sharks and other creatures that live in the ocean.

In all of the books you will learn that life in the wild is not easy. But you will also learn what people can do to help wildlife survive. So read on!